THE BEST OF WORLD SOCCER

THE BEST WOMEN'S PLAYERS OF WORLD SOCCER

BY CHRÖS MCDOUGALL

SportsZone
An Imprint of Abdo Publishing
abdobooks.com

abdobooks.com

Published by Abdo Publishing, a division of ABDO, PO Box 398166, Minneapolis, Minnesota 55439. Copyright © 2024 by Abdo Consulting Group, Inc. International copyrights reserved in all countries. No part of this book may be reproduced in any form without written permission from the publisher. SportsZone™ is a trademark and logo of Abdo Publishing.

Printed in the United States of America, North Mankato, Minnesota.
102023
012024

THIS BOOK CONTAINS RECYCLED MATERIALS

Cover Photo: Ezra Shaw/Allsport/Getty Images Sport/Getty Images
Interior Photos: Photo 12/Universal Images Group/Getty Images, 4–5; Fox Photos/Hulton Archive/Getty Images, 6; Thomas Cheng/AFP/Getty Images, 9, 13; Andy Lyons/Allsport/Hulton Archive/Getty Images, 10; Rick Stewart/Allsport/Getty Images Sport/Getty Images, 11, 14; Tom Shaw/Allsport/Getty Images Sport/Getty Images, 16–17; Jamie Squire/Getty Images Sport/Getty Images, 18; Mike Powell/Allsport/Getty Images Sport/Getty Images, 21; Roberto Schmidt/AFP/Getty Images, 23; Jeff Gross/Getty Images Sport/Getty Images, 24; Lars Baron/Bongarts/Getty Images, 26–27; Marcus Brandt/AFP/Getty Images, 28; Quality Sport Images/Getty Images Sport/Getty Images, 29; Pascal Guyot/AFP/Getty Images, 31; STR/AFP/Getty Images, 33; Daniel Roland/AFP/Getty Images, 34; Lars Baron/FIFA/Getty Images, 36–37; Stanley Chou/Getty Images Sport/Getty Images, 38; Christopher Lee/Getty Images Sport/Getty Images, 40; Thor Wegner/DeFodi Images/Getty Images, 43; Aitor Alcalde Colomer/Getty Images Sport/Getty Images, 44; Naomi Baker/Getty Images Sport/Getty Images, 45

Editor: Charlie Beattie
Series Designers: Karli Kruse and Joshua Olson

Library of Congress Control Number: 2023939432

Publisher's Cataloging-in-Publication Data

Names: McDougall, Chrös, author.
Title: The best women's players of world soccer / by Chrös McDougall
Description: Minneapolis, Minnesota: Abdo Publishing, 2024 | Series: The best of world soccer | Includes online resources and index.
Identifiers: ISBN 9781098292300 (lib. bdg.) | ISBN 9798384910244 (ebook)
Subjects: LCSH: Soccer--Juvenile literature. | Professional sports--Juvenile literature. | Women soccer players--Juvenile literature. | Soccer for women--Juvenile literature. | Soccer Teams--Juvenile literature. | Soccer--Records--Juvenile literature.
Classification: DDC 796.334--dc23

TABLE OF CONTENTS

CHAPTER 1
PIONEERS 4

CHAPTER 2
TAKING OVER 16

CHAPTER 3
GOING GLOBAL 26

CHAPTER 4
NEW WAVE 36

GLOSSARY 46
MORE INFORMATION 47
ONLINE RESOURCES 47
INDEX 48
ABOUT THE AUTHOR 48

CHAPTER 1

PIONEERS

With 11 players on each side, soccer requires great teamwork. A truly great player can have a massive impact for a team, however. And throughout the history of women's soccer, some superstars have stood especially tall. The pioneers of women's soccer turned the game from an

 Women's soccer became briefly popular in the early 1900s.

afterthought to a mainstream sport. Each generation of new players has emerged to take the game to the next level.

Soccer was still a young sport going into the 1900s. Though people had long been playing soccer-like games, many point to 1863 as the official beginning. That's when men's soccer clubs from around England came together to set official rules. Over the coming years, the sport began to grow. And by the 1920s, one of the most popular teams in England was the Dick, Kerr Ladies.

The team was made up of workers from a local munitions factory in Preston, England. With the country fighting in World War I (1914–1918), the team proved to be a welcome distraction. A crowd of 10,000 fans came out to see them play on Christmas Day in 1917. Eventually crowds reached five times that. One of the big reasons for the growing fan interest was a teenage scoring sensation named Lily Parr.

Parr was just 15 when she joined the team in 1920. Yet with her powerful left-footed shot, she quickly became a dangerous scorer. She reportedly once shot the ball so hard that a male goalkeeper broke his arm trying to save it. Parr scored routinely. She tallied 43 goals in her first year with the team. Fans across England were drawn to watch Parr and her team. However, the success would not last.

Lily Parr, *center*, goes up for a ball during a practice session for the Preston Ladies Football Club.

The Football Association (FA) governs soccer in England. After the war, the FA became concerned that women's teams were becoming too popular and taking attention away from the men's teams. So in 1921, the FA barred women from playing on its fields. This essentially banned women's soccer in England.

Parr and Dick, Kerr didn't go away entirely. The team eventually was renamed Preston Ladies and continued playing games when it could. Parr, who later became a nurse, continued playing until she was 45 years old. She reportedly scored nearly 1,000 goals while rarely missing a game. However, fans could only imagine what Parr might have done had she been given more chances.

FIGHTING FOR OPPORTUNITY

Parr and her English teammates were not the only women denied an opportunity during this time. Around the world, many viewed sports as being improper for women. As a result, some proud soccer countries, such as Germany, banned women from playing. Others simply refused to support the women's game. This led to many decades of women's soccer being hidden in the shadows—if it existed at all.

Attitudes toward women's soccer began slowly changing during the 1970s. By the 1980s, some countries were making real progress. The Scandinavian countries of Sweden and Norway were two of the sport's early leaders.

Sweden won the first European Championship in 1984. A 24-year-old forward named Pia Sundhage scored the winning goal in a penalty shootout. Sundhage was a versatile player for Sweden, able to play anywhere on the field. She was at her best when attacking the opposing goal, though. Sundhage scored 71 goals in 146 matches for Sweden. Her performance helped the nation finish third at the first Women's World Cup in 1991. Later she went on to a successful coaching career, including a stint as head coach of the US women's national team.

SUSANNE AUGUSTESEN
Italy hosted an unofficial women's world championship in 1970. Another tournament the next year in Mexico was even bigger. A crowd of 110,000 came out to the final. Susanne Augustesen, a 15-year-old forward, scored all three goals for Denmark in a 3–0 win over Mexico. It was Denmark's second win in a row, but the tournament did not continue after that year.

Norway's Linda Medalen, *left*, chases a loose ball against Sweden during the 1991 Women's World Cup.

Norway failed to qualify for the first European Championship. Three years later, Norway beat Sweden to win the second edition. Later in 1987, Linda Medalen joined Norway's national team. She broke into the top level of the sport as an elite goal scorer. As Medalen got older, she used her speed and experience to become a shutdown central defender. Medalen eventually became team captain and helped Norway remain a power into the 1990s.

THE WORLD STAGE

In August 1985, the US women's national team took the field for the first time at a tournament in Jesolo, Italy. Led by part-time coach Mike Ryan, the Americans played four matches. They lost three and tied one. It was a rough beginning.

The next year, Anson Dorrance was hired as the full-time coach for the team. He had built a powerhouse program at the University of North Carolina. With the national team, he introduced an aggressive new playing style. The US players prioritized fitness while playing a high press that left opponents with little time to make decisions.

Three forwards led the way. April Heinrichs, who had played for Dorrance at North Carolina, was named captain. She brought an ultracompetitive mentality that spread throughout the team. Fellow forward Carin Jennings could weave through opposing defenses with her masterful dribbling skills. Joining them on the forward line was Michelle Akers.

 **Carin Jennings of the United States scored the first hat trick in Women's World Cup history against Germany in 1991.**

Akers had just finished her freshman year at the University of Central Florida in 1985 when she got a letter inviting her to be on that first national team. "At first I had no idea what the

Michelle Akers scored the first-ever goal in US women's national team history during a game in 1985.

national team was," she said later. Akers had been a physical, tough-as-nails midfielder in college. With the national team she soon became a dominant forward. Combining strength, athleticism, and skill, she was relentless while attacking the opposing goal.

FIFA, which governs world soccer, had been holding a men's World Cup since 1930. Finally, in 1991, it created a women's tournament. By then, the US team had grown into a power. The players arrived in China for what is now considered the first Women's World Cup, and they dominated. In six games, the Americans gave up just five goals and scored 25. The final

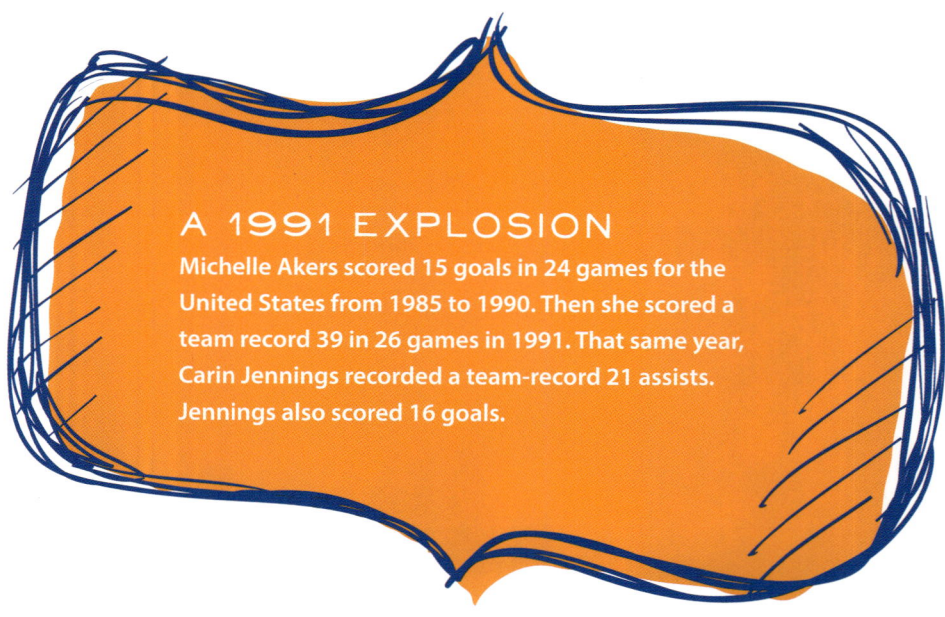

A 1991 EXPLOSION
Michelle Akers scored 15 goals in 24 games for the United States from 1985 to 1990. Then she scored a team record 39 in 26 games in 1991. That same year, Carin Jennings recorded a team-record 21 assists. Jennings also scored 16 goals.

pitted the United States and Norway against each other. Akers scored her ninth goal of the tournament early in the game.

Medalen scored for Norway to tie things up before halftime. It was still 1–1 with two minutes to go before stoppage time.

Julie Foudy, *left,* **Michelle Akers,** *center,* **and Carin Jennings of the United States celebrate with the championship trophy after defeating Norway in the 1991 World Cup final.**

In 1999 Michelle Akers became only the fourth player in international soccer history to score 100 goals.

A Norwegian defender stole a pass deep in her own end. Akers charged toward her. Flustered, the defender tried to pass back to the goalkeeper. Akers got there first. She tapped the ball into an open space, then cut back and beat the goalkeeper with a shot. Akers's 10th tally earned her the Golden Boot as the tournament's top scorer. Heinrichs and Jennings combined for 10 more goals, with Jennings earning the Golden Ball as the tournament's best player. Most importantly, the United States was the first Women's World Cup champion.

Knee injuries ended Heinrichs's career after that 1991 World Cup. She retired with 35 goals in 46 international games and later coached the US team. Jennings became Carin Gabarra after getting married. She played for the US team through 1996 before retiring with 56 goals in 119 games.

Akers, meanwhile, reinvented herself. Injuries and chronic fatigue syndrome took their toll on her physically. In her early years, she was the world's most dangerous goal scorer. To keep playing at an elite level, she moved to a less demanding defensive midfield role in the late 1990s. Competing with what new US coach Tony DiCicco called a "warrior mentality," she used her size, toughness, and smarts to snuff out opposing attacks. Akers retired after leading the Americans to victory on home soil in the 1999 World Cup. Shortly after, FIFA named her co-Women's Player of the Century.

CHAPTER 2

TAKING OVER

Hege Riise collected a pass in opposing territory, then quickly got to work. The Norwegian midfielder cut to her left, sending the ball between the legs of one German defender. Another tap of the ball sent it beyond the reach of a second defender's slide tackle. Then, when two more defenders

« **Hege Riise played in 188 international matches for Norway.**

hesitated, Riise ripped a long-range shot between them and into the net. Norway was playing Germany in the 1995 World Cup final. Riise's wonder goal in the 37th minute put her team up 1–0. Her teammate Marianne Pettersen sealed the 2–0 win just three minutes later.

Riise's World Cup career got off to a forgettable start. Facing host China in the first game of the World Cup in 1991, Riise and Norway fell 4–0. Norway ended up going to the final of that tournament. Then Riise led Norway to victory at the 1993 European Championship, the 1995 World Cup, and the 2000 Olympics. Her performance at the 1995 World Cup earned her the Golden Ball. By the time Riise retired from the national team in 2004, many considered her to be Norway's best-ever player.

THE FAB FIVE

Few paid any notice when three American teenagers stepped onto the field on August 3, 1987, in Tianjin, China. With the United States facing China in a pair of international friendlies, Joy Biefeld, 19, Mia Hamm, 15, and Kristine Lilly, 16, each made her national team debut in the 2–0 win. A year later, defender Brandi Chastain, 19, and midfielder Julie Foudy, 17, joined them on the team. Those players, eventually nicknamed

Julie Foudy scored 45 goals in 273 games as a member of the US women's national team.

"the Fab Five," went on to serve as the backbone of the US team for nearly two decades.

Biefeld, who later became Joy Fawcett, was a shutdown defender. Disciplined and consistent, she rarely committed fouls. And when opportunity arose, she could race up the field and join the attack. She ended her career with 27 international goals. Chastain joined Fawcett on the back line after starting her career as a forward. Her endless energy at left back made her a pest for opposing forwards.

Foudy and Lilly played in the midfield. An outspoken leader, Foudy became the team's captain. Lilly, who played on the outside, took over after Foudy retired. By the time Lilly retired in 2011, she had appeared in 354 games for the United States. No player, man or woman, had more international appearances.

The team's biggest star during this time, however, was Hamm. She did not score her first international goal until 1990. The next year, at age 19, she started five games and scored two goals at the first Women's World Cup. Hamm played mostly as a midfielder during the tournament. Before long, she moved to the forward line and became the game's most dangerous scorer. Hamm combined lightning speed with a delicate touch and a booming right foot. Over her career she scored 158 international goals. No player at the time, man or woman, had more. Along the way, Hamm also became the sport's most recognizable face while racking up major endorsement deals throughout the late 1990s and early 2000s. In doing so, Hamm became a pioneer for female athletes in all sports.

Behind new star athletes like Hamm and her teammates, women's sports grew tremendously during the 1990s. The Fab Five helped the United States win the first World Cup in 1991. They also led the US team to victory in the first Olympic women's soccer tournament, which took place in Atlanta in 1996. Their most famous moment came in the 1999 World Cup, which was also held in the United States.

SHOT STOPPER
Briana Scurry played 173 international games in goal for the United States between 1994 and 2008. She appeared in four Women's World Cups and two Olympics. Her save in the penalty shootout against China was key to the United States winning the 1999 World Cup. Scurry also won two Olympic gold medals.

After the sport attracted big crowds at the 1996 Olympics, World Cup organizers booked some of the country's biggest stadiums for 1999. Hamm was the star attraction. Though shy by nature, Hamm displayed fierce skills and a humble personality that appealed to fans. Huge crowds cheered for her and her teammates wherever they went. The biggest crowd yet was on hand for the final. More than 90,000 fans showed up at the Rose Bowl in California to watch the United States face China.

Michelle Akers once again proved to be the driving force

In addition to her 158 international goals, Mia Hamm also provided a record 144 assists for the United States.

for the US team. Playing the midfield "destroyer" role, she threw her body into every opportunity to break up opposing attacks. But after 90 minutes, and then 30 more of extra time, neither team had scored. The championship came down to a penalty shootout.

The fifth US shooter, Chastain, stepped to the spot with an opportunity to win the game. After drilling a left-footed shot into the corner of the net, she pulled off her shirt and fell to her knees as her teammates raced to celebrate with her. The moment instantly went down as one of the most iconic in US sports history.

The Fab Five continued to play together through 2004. That year Hamm, Fawcett, and Foudy retired. After winning an Olympic silver medal in 2000, they went out on top as Olympic gold medalists in 2004.

STARS OF CHINA

The US win at the 1999 World Cup became a landmark moment in American sports. That historic victory was hardly a given, though. In fact, many believed China would win that match. Skilled players such as midfielder Liu Ailing and goalie Gao Hong had helped the team become a power. But most importantly, China had Sun Wen. Many considered the crafty forward to be the world's best player.

Brandi Chastain of the United States celebrates after scoring the winning penalty kick against China in the 1999 Women's World Cup final.

Sun Wen chases the ball during a match against Ghana at the 2003 Women's World Cup.

China had been a tough opponent for the United States in the 1996 Olympic gold-medal game, with Sun scoring in China's 2–1 loss. Three years later, she was even better. Standing 5 feet, 4 inches tall, Sun was a world-class playmaker. Nothing seemed to rattle her on the field. And in 1999 she broke out as a dangerous scorer too. "She's just good in every aspect of the game," US defender Kate Sobrero said before the 1999 final.

Though Sun didn't score in that game, her seven goals tied for the tournament lead. She was also awarded the Golden Ball. Soon after, FIFA named her co-Women's Player of the Century, along with Akers. Sun retired in 2003, having scored 106 goals in 152 games for China.

CHAPTER 3

GOING GLOBAL

Germany had long been among the elite in women's soccer. From 1989 to 2001, it won five of the six European Championship tournaments. But the Germans had yet to win a global championship at the Women's World Cup or the Olympics. They finally broke through in 2003.

 Birgit Prinz won the Golden Boot at the 2003 Women's World Cup after leading all scorers at the tournament with seven goals.

Birgit Prinz grew up playing lots of sports. By her teenage years, she had dedicated herself to soccer. She was just 16 when she debuted with the German national team—and she scored the game-winning goal. From there the attacker developed into one of the world's premier players.

Prinz was 25 years old when the 2003 World Cup kicked off in the United States. And she was dominant. At 5-foot-10, she combined great size, athleticism, and scoring ability. This helped her win the Golden Ball and Golden Boot as Germany won its first Women's World Cup title. That year she also won the first of three consecutive Women's World Player of the Year awards.

Silke Rottenberg provided a steady presence in goal for Germany. The team's longtime goalie gave up just four goals in six games at the 2003 tournament. Injuries kept her out of the 2007 World Cup, but Germany had the perfect replacement in Nadine Angerer. Over six games at the tournament in China, Angerer didn't allow a goal. Her biggest save came in the final against Brazil. In the second half, Brazil was awarded a penalty kick. Angerer stuffed the shot from Brazilian star Marta to keep the score 1–0. Germany eventually won 2–0.

Prinz played on through the 2011 World Cup in Germany. Not long after a disappointing showing from the host nation,

Germany goalie Nadine Angerer directs her defense during the 2007 World Cup.

she retired having scored 128 goals in 214 international games. That included 14 in the World Cup, which was tied for the record. Angerer took over for Prinz as team captain in 2011. Known for her leadership and dedication to her craft, Angerer in 2013 became the first goalie—male or female—to be named World Player of the Year. After the 2015 World Cup in Canada, she retired with 146 international appearances. Both Prinz and Angerer also helped Germany win three Olympic bronze medals.

MARVELOUS MARTA

With a flick of her left foot, Marta unleashed a devastating attack. The United States was riding a 51-game unbeaten streak entering the 2007 World Cup semifinals. Three years earlier, the Americans had defeated Marta and Brazil in the 2004 Olympic gold-medal game. But in the rematch, Marta and Brazil didn't just get revenge; they humiliated the powerhouse US team.

Marta got the ball outside the corner of the US penalty area. With her back to the goal and a defender close, the Brazilian flicked the ball over her left shoulder. Then she cut to her right, ran around the US defender, and caught back up to the ball now inside the penalty area. A second US defender stepped into Marta's path. Marta's shifty dribble sent the defender lunging one way while the

In 2019 Marta became the first player, male or female, to score in five different World Cups.

Brazilian charged the other. Finally, with space to herself in the middle of the penalty area, Marta slammed a low shot into the US goal. The goal secured Brazil's 4–0 victory. It also confirmed Marta's status as the best player in the world.

Born in the small town of Dois Riachos, Brazil, Marta grew up in a country famous for its great soccer players. But those players were all men. When Marta was young, people tried to stop her and other girls from playing. She was determined, though. She'd create a ball using old grocery bags and dribble it around Dois Riachos. She eventually joined a boys' team.

Marta started her professional career with Brazilian club Vasco da Gama at age 14. At age 17, she debuted with Brazil's national team in 2003. After four years playing in her home

AFRICAN STARS

Africa has trailed other parts of the world in growing women's soccer. Some skilled players have emerged from the continent, however. Perpetua Nkwocha was a midfielder and forward from Nigeria. She won four African Women's Player of the Year awards from 2004 to 2011. That was a record until fellow Nigerian Asisat Oshoala, a forward, won her fifth in 2022.

Brazil midfielder Formiga, *right*, became the oldest player in Women's World Cup history in 2019, when she played in the tournament at age 41.

country, Marta moved to a professional team in Sweden. By then she had grown into a 5-foot-2 forward who could do it all.

Other countries offered more support to women's soccer players. Yet many skilled players emerged from Brazil. Reliable midfielder Formiga played in a record seven World Cups and seven Olympics before retiring in 2021. Another midfielder, Sissi, tied for the most goals scored at the 1999 World Cup. Forward Cristiane made her debut in 2003. Twenty years later, she was still a goal-scoring threat.

Behind these players, Brazil enjoyed some great successes. The team finished as runner-up at the 2007 World Cup. It won Olympic silver medals in 2004 and 2008. The one thing Brazil didn't win was a global championship.

Individually, however, no woman has claimed as many individual honors as Marta. Her technical abilities on the ball often left defenders looking foolish. Her vision and creativity elevated her teammates. And despite her smaller size, she could overwhelm opponents with her speed and toughness. This combination of skills led to her winning a record six Women's World Player of the Year awards between 2006 and 2018. At one point during that stretch, Marta took home the award five straight years.

JAPAN'S CHAMPIONS

Few people were talking about Japan as a contender going into the 2011 World Cup. No Asian country had ever won the tournament. Meanwhile, the country had been rocked by a tragic earthquake and tsunami in March 2011. The team had talent, though. And no player shone like Homare Sawa.

The midfielder scored four goals in her international debut as a 15-year-old in 1993. She made her World Cup debut in 1995. However, for many years she was overshadowed by stars on better teams. That changed in a big way in 2011. At that

Cristiane, *left*, and Marta celebrate a Brazil goal during the 2008 Olympics in Beijing, China.

Homare Sawa celebrates after scoring Japan's game-tying goal in extra time against the United States in the 2011 World Cup final.

year's World Cup in Germany, Sawa's tireless effort made her a key contributor on offense and defense.

In a surprise, Sawa led Japan to the final against the United States. After playing to a 1–1 tie, the Americans took the lead in extra time. Then, in the 117th minute, Japan got a corner kick. Slicing across the goal area, Sawa perfectly flicked the ball behind her and into the goal. Japan won in a shootout. Afterward, Sawa swept the tournament's Golden Ball and Golden Boot awards. She was also named Women's World Player of the Year. The next year, Sawa led Japan to the Olympic silver medal. She retired after another World Cup runner-up finish in 2015 as an icon in her home country.

KELLY THE LIONESS

England emerged as a power in the women's game during the 2010s. Kelly Smith helped set that foundation. A lethal forward, she scored her first international goal at age 17 in 1995. Over the next 20 years she added 45 more. No woman scored more for England. Smith also enjoyed a successful club career, notably with Arsenal of London.

CHAPTER 4

NEW WAVE

Mia Hamm played in her last major tournament for the United States at the 2004 Olympics in Athens, Greece. As she exited the stage, a new American star showed she was ready to take over. In the gold-medal match, the United States and Brazil went into extra time tied 1–1. With a shootout

 Over her 15 years with the US national team, Abby Wambach won a Women's World Cup title as well as a pair of Olympic gold medals.

looming, 24-year-old forward Abby Wambach rose into the air over a defender. Then she drilled a header into the goal to secure the gold medal.

That was one of 184 international goals Wambach scored in her career. At the time of her retirement, no man or woman had scored more. And like the 2004 goal in Athens, many of them were big ones. At 5 feet, 11 inches, Wambach was particularly dangerous in the air. That showed in the quarterfinals of the 2011 World Cup. In the 122nd minute, Brazil was seconds away from securing a 2–1 win. Then American winger Megan Rapinoe sent a desperation cross 45 yards through the air.

SUPER SINCLAIR

Christine Sinclair first suited up for Canada in 2000, and she began scoring soon after. In January 2020, Sinclair scored her 185th goal. That moved her past Abby Wambach for the all-time international scoring record. The goal came in Sinclair's 290th game for Canada. And one year later, Sinclair led Canada to its first major championship at the Olympics.

Alex Morgan, *left*, and Carli Lloyd, *right*, were part of an incredible US attack during the 2010s.

Wambach drove the ball into the net. It was the latest goal ever scored in World Cup play. More importantly, the goal tied the game. The United States went on to win in a shootout.

Wambach was at the tail end of her career at the 2015 World Cup. This time she played a supporting role for the talented US team. Carli Lloyd and Alex Morgan were two of the world's most dangerous forwards. And nobody thrived in big moments like Lloyd. The New Jersey native had already scored the game-winning goals in the 2008 and 2012 Olympic gold-medal games. Facing Japan in the 2015 final, Lloyd scored off a corner kick in the third minute. Two minutes later, she tapped in another goal. Then, in the 16th minute, she launched a shot from near midfield that sailed over the goalie for a hat trick. The Americans went on to win 5–2.

By the 2019 World Cup, Lloyd was a substitute player for the US team. She might have started on any other team in the world. But Morgan, Rapinoe, and Tobin Heath made up a world-class forward line. Morgan was a lethal finisher. That showed when she scored five goals against Thailand in the group stage. Morgan struck with speed and precision. Rapinoe and Heath brought creativity from the wings. The United States repeated as champions. With six goals and two assists, Rapinoe won the Golden Ball and Golden Boot.

Goal scorers get a lot of attention. Americans in other positions also played key roles in the team's success. Goalie Hope Solo allowed just one goal in six games at the 2015 World Cup. Her acrobatic saves helped her become the first player to record 100 international shutouts. Julie Ertz went from playing center back to central midfield. In either position, her physical shutdown play made her a force. Hard-nosed Becky Sauerbrunn served as an anchor on the defense for more than 200 games. Crystal Dunn, meanwhile, is a star attacker with her club team and a world-class left back for the US team.

Lyon forward Ada Hegerberg, *center*, dribbles between two defenders during a Champions League match in 2017.

EUROPEAN STARS

Striker Ada Hegerberg led Norway's professional league in scoring as a 16-year-old in 2011. After two more prolific years, she moved to French club Olympique Lyonnais, commonly known as Lyon, the dominant team in women's club soccer. Hegerberg announced her arrival by scoring 26 goals in 22 league games. In 2018 she was awarded the prestigious Ballon d'Or given to the best women's player in the world.

Hegerberg showed that Norway was still a leader in women's soccer. However, that list of top countries continues to grow. When the Women's World Cup started in 1991, the

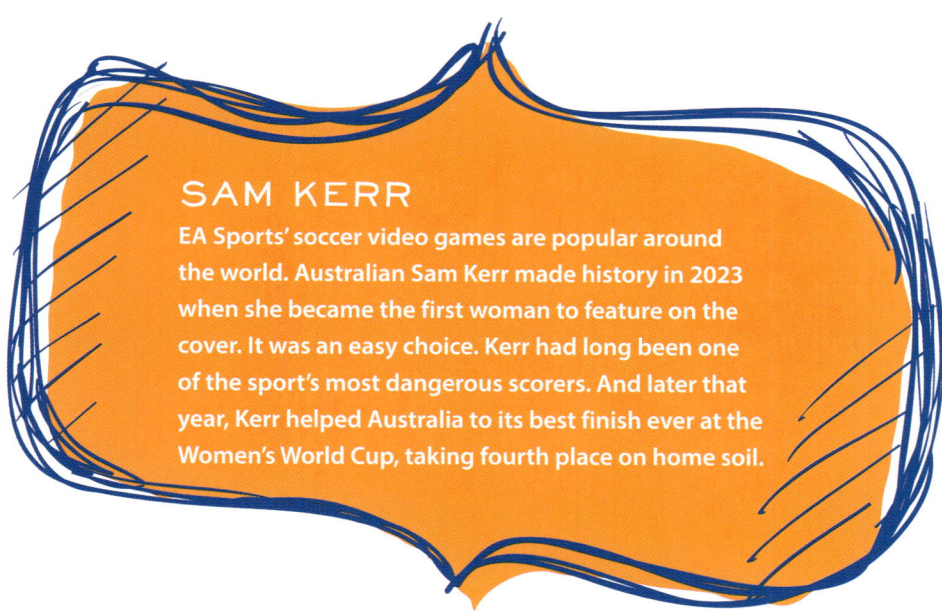

SAM KERR
EA Sports' soccer video games are popular around the world. Australian Sam Kerr made history in 2023 when she became the first woman to feature on the cover. It was an easy choice. Kerr had long been one of the sport's most dangerous scorers. And later that year, Kerr helped Australia to its best finish ever at the Women's World Cup, taking fourth place on home soil.

tournament had 12 teams. By 2023 it had grown to 32. As more and more countries support women's soccer, more of them are producing star players. Some of the strongest growth has come in Europe.

France didn't qualify for a Women's World Cup until 2003, and then it missed out again in 2007. Four years later, France took fourth place. Several talented players arose to make France a contender. Few had the impact of Wendie Renard. Born and raised on the Caribbean island of Martinique, she moved to France as a teenager. There she developed into an imposing 6-foot-2-inch center back. Renard also anchored Lyon to its 15th French league title and eighth European title in 2022.

To the north, the Netherlands qualified for its first Women's World Cup in 2015. Two years later, young midfielder/forward Lieke Martens enjoyed a breakout performance at the 2017 European Championship. Her speed and playmaking from the outside helped the Dutch win all six games—and their first major tournament. Martens scored a goal in the 4–2 win over Denmark in the final. Her even younger strike partner, Vivianne Miedema, added two more. And two years after that, the pair lifted the Netherlands to the 2019 World Cup final.

Soccer was invented in England, but then the FA banned women from playing. A century later, the English women's team became one of the best in the world. Star players such as

Defender Wendie Renard made her first appearance for the French national team in 2011.

Lucy Bronze were a big part of that. Her versatility makes her a threat all over the field, though she's at her best as a right back who can charge upfield and join the attack. In 2022 England hosted the European Championship. Nobody had more goals or assists there than Beth Mead. In front of a record home crowd of 87,000, England beat Germany 2–1 in the final. Then, one year later, England reached its first Women's World Cup final.

In that game, England ran into another fast-rising power. Spain made its first Women's World Cup appearance in 2015. Going into the 2023 tournament, Spain had never advanced beyond the round of 16. But players like Alexia Putellas were showing that Spanish women's soccer could be a force internationally. The midfield

« **Alexia Putellas became the fourth woman to be named World Player of the Year multiple times after winning the award in 2021 and 2022.**

Lucy Bronze celebrates after scoring for England in the semifinals of the 2022 European Championship.

playmaker led her club team, Barcelona, to its first European title in 2021. Then she became the first Spanish woman to win the Ballon d'Or, doing so in 2021 and 2022.

Though Putellas was slowed by injuries at the 2023 World Cup, talented teammates such as Aitana Bonmatí stepped up. Bonmatí's skill and vision helped Spain dominate the midfield on the way to its first Women's World Cup title. It was another example of how, after the women's game was held back for so long, the sport's stars continue to make up for lost time.

GLOSSARY

ASSIST
A pass, shot, or deflection that leads directly to a teammate's goal.

CLUB
The team a player competes with outside of his or her national team.

ENDORSEMENT
A deal in which an athlete promotes a company in exchange for the company's products or money.

EXTRA TIME
Two 15-minute periods added to a tournament game if the score is tied at the end of regulation.

FRIENDLY
An exhibition match that is not part of league play or a tournament.

HAT TRICK
Three or more goals by the same player in one game.

HIGH PRESS
When the forwards push forward to put pressure on the opposing team, making it harder for them to move upfield with the ball.

PENALTY AREA
The box in front of the goal where a player is granted a penalty kick if he or she is fouled.

PENALTY KICK
A play in which a shooter faces a goalkeeper alone; it is used to decide tied tournament games or as a result of a foul.

RETIRE
To end one's career.

SHOOTOUT
A series of penalty kicks held after extra time to decide who wins a game.

STOPPAGE TIME
Also known as injury time, a number of minutes tacked onto the end of a half for stoppages that occurred during play from injuries, free kicks, and goals.

VERSATILE
Able to perform many different roles or functions.

WONDER GOAL
An extraordinary or unexpected goal.

MORE INFORMATION

BOOKS

Carothers, Thomas. *Women's World Cup Heroes*. Minneapolis, MN: Abdo Publishing, 2019.

Hanlon, Luke. *Alex Morgan*. Minneapolis, MN: Abdo Publishing, 2024.

Hewson, Anthony K. *GOATs of Soccer*. Minneapolis, MN: Abdo Publishing, 2022.

ONLINE RESOURCES

To learn more about women's soccer, please visit **abdobooklinks.com** or scan this QR code. These links are routinely monitored and updated to provide the most current information available.

INDEX

Akers, Michelle, 10–13, 15, 21, 25
Angerer, Nadine, 27–28
Augustesen, Susanne, 8

Bonmatí, Aitana, 45
Bronze, Lucy, 44

Chastain, Brandi, 17, 19, 22
Cristiane, 31

Dunn, Crystal, 39

Ertz, Julie, 39

Fawcett, Joy (née Biefeld), 17, 19, 22
Formiga, 31
Foudy, Julie, 17, 19, 22

Gabarra, Carin (née Jennings), 10, 12, 15
Gao Hong, 22

Hamm, Mia, 17, 19–22, 36
Heath, Tobin, 39
Hegerberg, Ada, 41
Heinrichs, April, 10, 15

Kerr, Sam, 41

Lilly, Kristine, 17, 19
Liu Ailing, 22
Lloyd, Carli, 38–39

Marta, 27, 29–32
Martens, Lieke, 42
Mead, Beth, 44
Medalen, Linda, 9, 13
Miedema, Vivianne, 42
Morgan, Alex, 38–39

Nkwocha, Perpetua, 30

Oshoala, Asisat, 30

Parr, Lily, 5, 7
Pettersen, Marianne, 17
Prinz, Birgit, 27–28
Putellas, Alexia, 44–45

Rapinoe, Megan, 37, 39
Renard, Wendie, 42
Riise, Hege, 16–17
Rottenberg, Silke, 27

Sauerbrunn, Becky, 39
Sawa, Homare, 32, 35
Scurry, Brianna, 20
Sinclair, Christine, 37
Sissi, 31
Smith, Kelly, 35
Sobrero, Kate, 25
Solo, Hope, 39
Sun Wen, 22, 25
Sundhage, Pia, 8

Wambach, Abby, 37–38

ABOUT THE AUTHOR

Chrös McDougall is an author, editor, and sportswriter who regularly covers soccer as well as Olympic and Paralympic sports. He's reported on the US women's soccer team, including at the 2021 Olympics in Tokyo, Japan, and Carli Lloyd's farewell game later that year. He lives in Minneapolis with his wife, his soccer-loving son and daughter, and an occasionally fierce boxer named Eira.